Write Better Sentences and Paragraphs

Level 5
English

Welcome to studySMART!

Write Better Sentences and Paragraphs provides opportunities for the systematic consolidation and further development of your child's writing skills from word to sentence to paragraph.

It can be a challenge to help children extend their writing skills. The fun and functional topics and variety of engaging exercises in this book will both stimulate and encourage your child to develop the necessary skills to advance as an independent writer. As your child encounters a variety of language and text features, they will learn to select and use the appropriate vocabulary, language structures and techniques for their writing. Your child will also learn to plan, write, proofread and further improve their writing.

Every section targets a specific skill and there is a section at the end of the book with test preparation tips, self-prompting hints, and common editing symbols.

How to use this book?

1. Introduce the target writing skill at the top of the page to your child.

2. Let your child complete the exercises.

3. Reinforce and extend your child's learning with the tips and activities in the To Parents note, where there is one, at the bottom of the page.

4. Refer to the Test Preparation Tips, Self-Prompting Hints, and Self-Evaluation Checklist to consolidate learning.

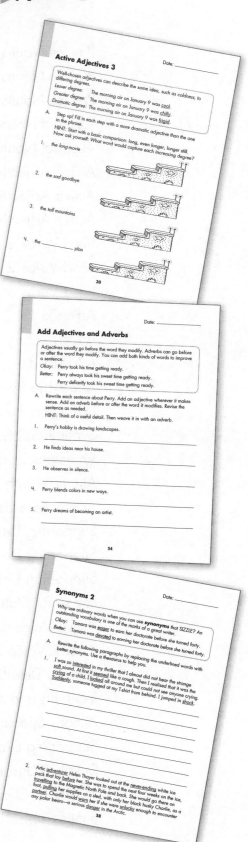

Contents

Precise Nouns 1 6–7

Precise Nouns 2 8–9

Precise Nouns 3 10–11

Abstract Nouns 1 12–13

Abstract Nouns 2 14–15

Active Adjectives 1 16–17

Active Adjectives 2 18–19

Active Adjectives 3 20–21

Vivid Verbs 1 22–23

Vivid Verbs 2 24–25

Vivid Verbs 3 26–27

Adverbs 1 28–29

Adverbs 2 30–31

Adverbs 3 32–33

Add Adjectives and Adverbs 34–35

Synonyms 1 36–37

Synonyms 2 38–39

Antonyms 40

Alternate with Antonyms 41–43

Active Advertising 44–45

Supporting Details 1 46–47

Supporting Details 2 48–49

Supporting Details 3 50–51

Facts and Statistics 52–53

Active Voice 54–55

Passive Voice 56–57

Sensory Details Diagram 58–59

Incidents and Anecdotes 60–61

Actions Speak Louder 62–63

Supporting Examples 64–65

Details Diagram 66–67

Making a Choice 68–69

Similes 1 70–71

Similes 2 72–73

Metaphors 1 74–75

Metaphors 2 76–77

Alliteration Headlines 78–79

Onomatopoeia 1 80–81

Onomatopoeia 2 82–83

Idioms 1 84–85

Idioms 2 86–87

Collocations 88–89

Exaggerate to Elaborate 90–91

Dialogue Details 92–93

Getting Ideas 94–95

Character Planner 96–97

Setting the Scene 98–99

Plotting 100–101

Build a Story 102–103

My Autobiography 104–105

Biographical Sketch 106–107

Select a Sentence 108–109

Vary Sentence Types 110–111

Vary Sentence Length 112–113

Making a List 114–115

How Things Work 116–117

Cut the Clutter 118–119

Elaborating Without Repeating 120–121

Identifying the Technique 122–123

Test Prep Tips 124

Common Editing Symbols 125

Self-Prompting Hints 126

Answers 127–128

Precise Nouns 1

Nouns are naming words. **Precise** or **exact nouns** name more exactly. Some nouns name persons, places or things. Some nouns name ideas. Use better naming words to make your writing more clear.

A. Categorize the nouns in the box below by completing the table.

Red panda	Bottlenose dolphin	Fennec fox	basketball
Central Park	Yellowstone National Park	integrity	baseball
Nature reserve	Shetland pony	kindness	strength
Art museum	lecturer	banker	cab driver
aerobics instructor	football field	basketball court	pride
referee	tennis court	Striped dolphin	Red fox

Category	Precise Nouns
Things / Animals	
Places	
Persons	
Ideas	

Can you think of more examples of precise nouns? Add other examples of precise nouns in the table above.

There are different kinds of nouns. Some nouns are **proper nouns** which name a specific person, thing or place. There are also **collective nouns** that are used to refer to a group of items.

B. Categorize the nouns in the table below. Then add other proper nouns you can think of to complete the table.

| Mr Tenney | Eiffel Tower | Beijing | Paris |
| Berlin | Mother Teresa | Prince William | Great Wall of China |

Common Nouns	Proper Nouns
Capital cities	
Landmarks	
People	

C. Complete the list below with collective nouns. Use the words in the box.

| herd | flock | team | band | gang | choir |

1. a _____ of cattle

2. a _____ of players

3. a _____ of birds

4. a _____ of singers

5. a _____ of thieves

6. a _____ of musicians

Precise Nouns 2

Nouns are naming words. **Precise** or **exact nouns** name more exactly.

Okay: That <u>sound</u> will calm the baby.

Better: That <u>lullaby</u> will calm the baby.

A. Make each sentence better. Look in the box for a better noun. Rewrite the sentence using the more precise noun.

> mansion   Main Street   music producer   singers   limousine

1. The rich family lives in a large <u>house</u>.

   _____

2. The chauffeur drives Mr Simpson around in a <u>car</u>.

   _____

3. They lived on <u>that street.</u>

   _____

4. Mr Simpson is a famous <u>person</u>.

   _____

5. He enjoys working with young <u>people</u>.

   _____

B.   HINT: Make a picture in your mind. Pick a precise noun to focus the picture.

1.   The best part of last night's meal was the <u>dessert</u>.

_____

2.   Use that <u>stuff</u> to make yourself look older.

_____

3.   Our old <u>pet</u> lived with us for 12 years.

_____

4.   The <u>jewel</u> fell out of Mom's ring.

_____

5.   The family trip to that <u>spot</u> was amazing.

_____

6.   Every year we hold Field Day at the same <u>place</u>.

_____

7.   I can't believe I caught that <u>fish</u> myself!

_____

8.   The <u>man</u> got a job on an offshore oil rig.

_____

To parents Challenge your child to list ten precise nouns that can be used to name a friend or family member.

Precise Nouns 3

Thing is a noun, but it is not a precise noun. The word *thing* is vague and hardly has much meaning.

Vague: Did you read that <u>thing</u>?

Precise: Did you read that <u>brochure</u>?

A.   Write three different precise nouns to replace every *thing*.

HINT: Be sure that each of the precise nouns will make the question clear.

1.   Can one *THING* hold all seven of them?

2.   Did you taste that *THING* she cooked?

3.   Have you memorized the *THING* yet?

4.   How tall can one *THING* grow?

5.   Is your *THING* all set for the show?

6.   What does that silly *THING* actually do?

7.   When will that *THING* be ready to use?

8.   Why does he want this *THING* anyway?

9.   Will you read that *THING* aloud to me?

10. Would you sing one *THING* for us?

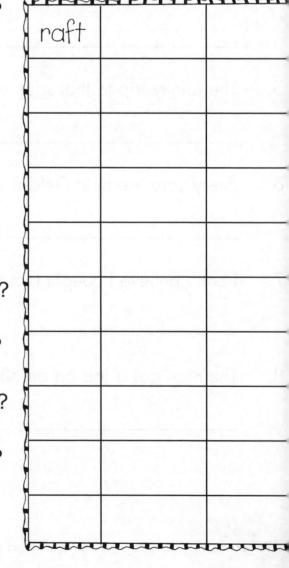

raft		

When you use the same words over and over in your writing, it becomes less effective and expressive. Overused and imprecise words should be replaced.

B. Replace some of the overused nouns in the sentences below with your own precise nouns. Rewrite the sentences. You do not have to replace every single instance of the noun.

1. She drove a small white car. Her father gave her that car as a birthday present because she has always loved that car.

_____

_____

2. Cheryl has a pet that she cherishes. Her pet is like her best friend. Whenever she is unhappy, her pet cheers her up and makes her laugh.

_____

_____

C. Replace the underlined imprecise phrases with precise nouns.

1. The woman who is interviewing the famous singer is my aunt.

_____

_____

2. My grandparents used to live on a place where they rear sheep and cows.

_____

_____

Abstract Nouns 1

Abstract nouns are naming words that cannot be experienced through the five senses. They name invisible qualities, characteristics, feelings, attitudes or values.

A. Categorize the following abstract nouns by completing the table. Then add three more abstract nouns in each category.

love	justice	anger	knowledge	faith
fear	sympathy	hatred	bravery	loyalty
honesty	thought	culture	compassion	courage

Categories	Abstract nouns
Qualities	
Feelings	
Ideas / Concepts	

B. Form abstract nouns using the words in brackets.

1. _____ (friend)   6. _____ (wise)

2. _____ (confide)   7. _____ (kind)

3. _____ (honest)   8. _____ (free)

4. _____ (brilliant)   9. _____ (good)

5. _____ (real)   10. _____ (child)

C.   Each of the sentences below is incomplete. Add *any* abstract noun that makes sense.

HINT: Pretend you're an actor. What feeling would fit each scene?

1.   Polly overcame her feelings of _____ to give a thrilling speech.

2.   Some have worked for generations to solve the problem of _____.

3.   After the furious storm, town residents expressed their deep _____.

4.   Because of his _____, Jacob seems to have the makings of a fine leader.

5.   It's always hard for children to control their _____ as the holidays draw near.

6.   The artist tried to capture the remarkable _____ of the region in her landscapes.

7.   How do people find the _____ they need to take risks for their beliefs?

8.   "I'm glad I had my camera. I captured that look of total _____ on her face!"

9.   Standing beside Niagara Falls reminds us of the breathtaking _____ of nature.

10.   "It was your _____ that allowed the dog to get out of the yard and run away!"

Abstract Nouns 2

Transform each of the sentences below by including an abstract noun from the box. The meaning of the sentence must remain unchanged.

E.g. *The exhausted athlete <u>was unsure</u> if he could complete the race.*

*The exhausted athlete had **doubts** <u>about whether he could complete the race.</u>*

accident	duty	education	enmity	grief
memory	liberty	prerequisite	zenith	success

1. I <u>do not have the right</u> to discuss Lucy's personal matter.

   I am not at _____

   _____

2. Nina had no appetite for food because she was <u>saddened</u> by her dog's death.

   Overcome with _____

   _____

3. Please write down the address lest you <u>forget</u>.

   _____

   lest your _____ you.

4. A teacher is <u>obliged</u> to discipline her students when they misbehave.

   It is a teacher's _____

   _____

5. All candidates who apply for this position <u>must be</u> fluent in Japanese.

It is a _____

_____

6. Many children in the world cannot afford <u>to go to school</u>.

Many children _____

_____

7. Dr Hawks <u>peaked</u> in his chosen field of study at the relatively young age of 36.

Dr Hawks reached the _____

_____

8. Her classmates <u>had planned for</u> Tina to get into trouble with Mrs Johnson.

It was by no _____

_____

9. Everyone knows that Malathy and Elaine <u>are hostile</u> towards each other.

The _____

_____ well-known.

10. Only if we persevere, can we expect to <u>triumph</u>.

_____

_____ only if we persevere.

Active Adjectives 1

Adjectives are words that describe, or modify nouns or pronouns. Adjectives add details to create an impact. Use active adjectives to make your writing more lively and expressive.

A.   Can you think of different words to describe a song? Complete the graphic organizer. Use the questions to help you.

What sound did the song have?
_____
_____
_____

What language was the song in?
_____
_____
_____

song

How did the song make you feel?
_____
_____
_____

What was the musical style of the song?
_____
_____
_____

B. Pick one of these nouns: ASTRONAUT   DANCER   DOCTOR
                                ATHLETE   SCIENTIST CHEATER

Write it in the center of the word web. Fill the web with adjectives
to describe the noun.

HINT: Adjectives easily answer questions like *Which one? What kind?
How many?*

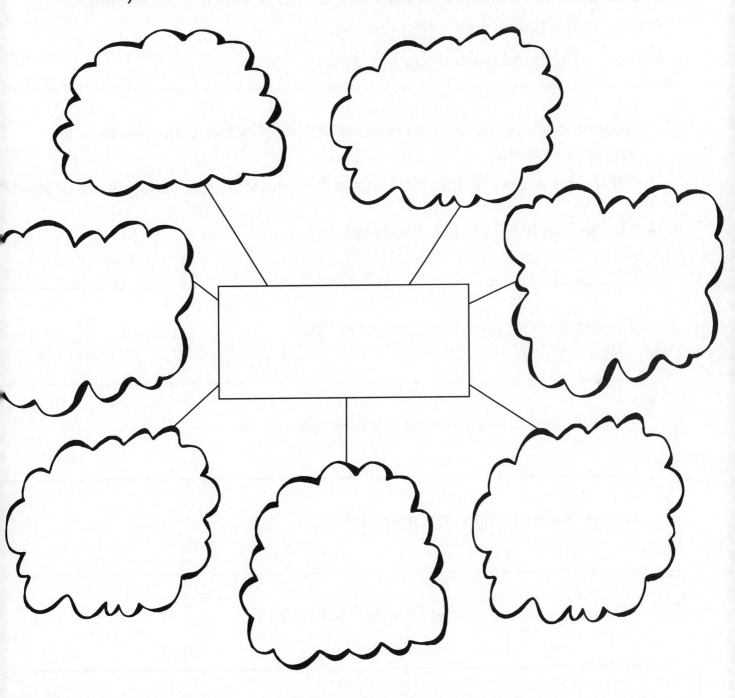

To parents   Ask your child to draw a new word web and fill it with adjectives to modify another noun from the
             list provided.

17

Active Adjectives 2

It is important to use **active adjectives** in your writing. Adjectives like *fine* or *cute* are often overused and do little to add details to your writing.

Boring: The band gave a <u>fine</u> concert.

Better: The band gave a <u>rousing</u> concert.

A. Rewrite each sentence. Use a more active, effective adjective than the empty one given.

HINT: Use sensory details. How would the noun look, feel, taste, sound, or smell?

1. His garden is full of such *fine* roses.

   _____

2. The amusement park has some *cute* rides.

   _____

3. Helen baked a *fine* cake for my birthday.

   _____

4. Mugsy learned some *cute* new tricks.

   _____

5. "Please wear *fine* clothes tonight," said Kevin.

   _____

6. That *cute* cartoon made me laugh out loud.

   _____

To make your writing more interesting, you can add two or more adjectives before a noun to tell more about it. However, the adjectives must be placed in a certain order: quality – size – age – shape – color – type.

Okay:　　She wore a pink dress. It was pretty. It was made of silk.

Better:　　She wore a pretty pink silk dress.

B.　Write a sentence containing the given noun and adjectives in the right order.

1.　Noun: house　　　Adjectives: grey, concrete, ugly

_____

2.　Noun: haversack　Adjectives: oversized, leather, black

_____

3.　Noun: lady　　　　Adjectives: slim, elegant, Japanese, young

_____

4.　Noun: cat　　　　Adjectives: Persian, white, fluffy, small

_____

C.　Now write a description of a noun of your choice using at least three adjectives in your sentence.

_____

_____

_____

To parents　Ask your child to write a sentence for each of these empty adjectives: *nice, good* and *bad*. Then replace each empty adjective with more effective adjectives.

Active Adjectives 3

Well-chosen adjectives can describe the same idea, such as *coldness*, to differing degrees.

Lesser degree: The morning air on January 9 was <u>cool</u>.

Greater degree: The morning air on January 9 was <u>chilly</u>.

Dramatic degree: The morning air on January 9 was <u>frigid</u>.

A.   Step up! Fill in each step with a more dramatic adjective than the one in the phrase.

HINT: Start with a basic comparison: long, even longer, longer still. Now ask yourself: What word would capture each increasing degree?

1.   the *long* movie

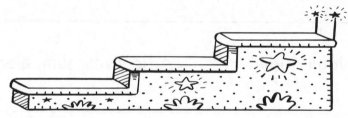

2.   the *sad* goodbye

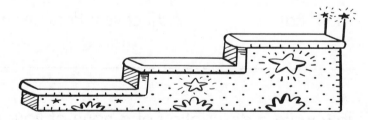

3.   the *tall* mountains

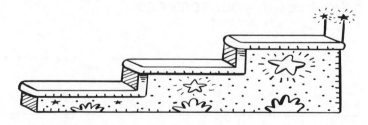

4.   the _____ plan

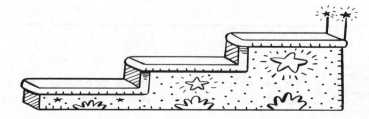

B. Create more vivid descriptions by replacing the underlined adjectives with more active adjectives.

1. The new teacher was <u>nice</u> and <u>pleasant</u>. She wore a <u>simple</u> yellow dress and tied her hair in a braid. She was <u>small</u> and <u>short</u> but she had a <u>loud</u> voice.

_____

_____

_____

2. The <u>nice, big</u> house stood by itself on a <u>small</u> hill. There was a path leading to the <u>scary</u> metal gate in front of the house. Beyond the gate was a <u>pretty</u> garden filled with all kinds of flowers.

_____

_____

_____

3. The man looked <u>scary</u>. He had a <u>frightening</u> stare that made my legs turn to jelly. His <u>old, dirty</u> clothes looked like they had been stolen and gave off a <u>bad</u> smell.

_____

_____

_____

Vivid Verbs 1

Verbs express action. **Vivid verbs** help bring the action to life.

A. Fill each column with vivid verbs that improve on the dull verbs at the top. Be creative! Think of fresh, exciting visual verbs.

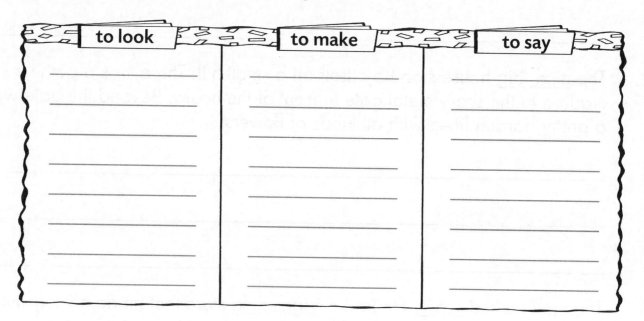

to look	to make	to say

B. Now, replace the verbs in the sentences below with alternative verbs to replace the underlined verbs. You may use some of the words that you came up with.

1. She <u>looked</u> behind her quickly to see if the man was still following her.

_____

2. The little boy <u>made</u> the toy robot all by himself and he was pleased.

_____

3. They <u>said</u> the word quietly, worried that someone might overhear them.

_____

C. Fill each column with vivid verbs that improve on the dull verbs at the top.
Be creative! Think of fresh, exciting visual verbs.

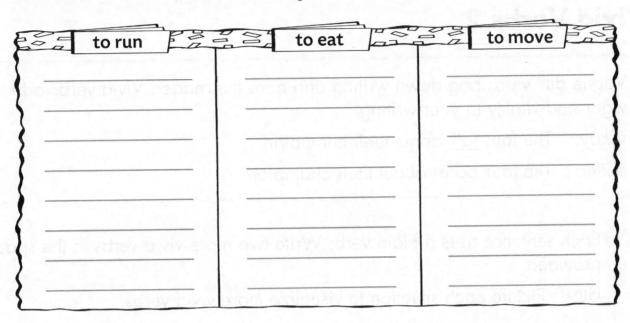

to run	to eat	to move

D. Now, write a short text using the words that you have come up with in the
table above to describe a situation when you were in a rush.

_____

_____

_____

_____

_____

_____

_____

To parents Ask your child to create more columns and collect vivid verbs for *do* and *take*.

Vivid Verbs 2

> Vague dull verbs bog down writing and bore the reader. Vivid verbs add vigor and vitality to your writing.
>
> *Okay:*   The fans <u>talk</u> about their champion.
>
> *Better:*   The fans <u>boast</u> about their champion.

A.   Each sentence uses a plain verb. Write two more vivid verbs in the space provided.

HINT: Picture each situation to visualize more vivid verbs.

1.   The runners <u>run</u> to the finish line.

_____

2.   Marcus <u>looks</u> at the scoreboard.

_____

3.   He <u>thinks</u> about what his coach said.

_____

4.   He feels his heart <u>go</u> inside his chest.

_____

5.   At last, the starting horn <u>sounds</u>.

_____

6.   Marcus <u>moves</u> as fast as he can.

_____

7.   Sports reporters <u>take</u> notes for their stories.

_____

B. Complete the following sentences with vivid verbs to illustrate the meaning in brackets.

1. The thief _____ from one end of the market to the other.
   (ran very quickly)

2. Penny _____ over the issue before coming to a decision.
   (thought for a long time)

3. Melody _____ over her table and wept.
   (sit down in a sad-looking manner)

4. They managed to _____ the bag back from the other team.
   (grab quickly)

5. The old man _____ as he walked because his feet hurt.
   (make sickly sounds)

6. The baby _____ pitifully as he was hungry.
   (cry loudly)

7. Sheena _____ when someone came up from behind her.
   (scream loudly)

8. Tina _____ that she would be withdrawing from the race.
   (said loudly)

9. The teacher _____ at her students as they were too rowdy.
   (shout loudly)

10. Ben _____ across the hall to show off
    (walk in a slow and purposeful manner)
    his new clothes.

To parents Ask your child to think of other vivid verbs that could replace the ones in the sentences above.

Vivid Verbs 3

A. Read the following passage. It is full of bland, lifeless verbs. Replace at least ten dull and overused verbs with vivid and more vibrant ones.

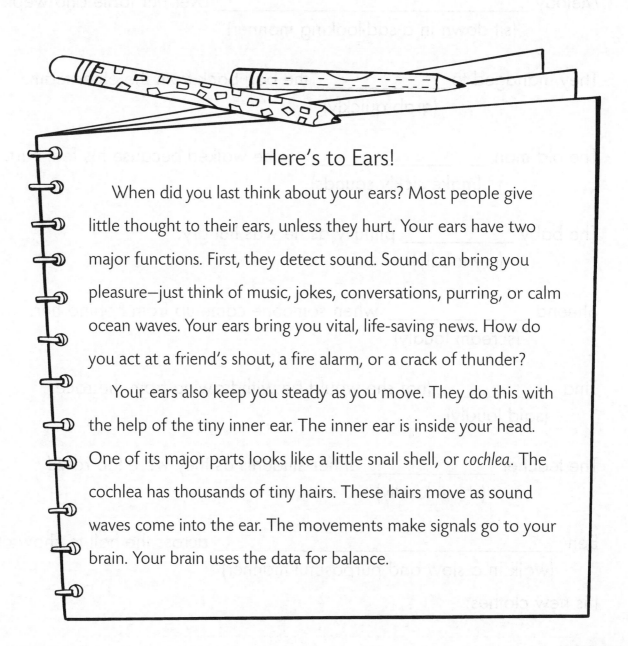

Here's to Ears!

When did you last think about your ears? Most people give little thought to their ears, unless they hurt. Your ears have two major functions. First, they detect sound. Sound can bring you pleasure—just think of music, jokes, conversations, purring, or calm ocean waves. Your ears bring you vital, life-saving news. How do you act at a friend's shout, a fire alarm, or a crack of thunder?

Your ears also keep you steady as you move. They do this with the help of the tiny inner ear. The inner ear is inside your head. One of its major parts looks like a little snail shell, or *cochlea*. The cochlea has thousands of tiny hairs. These hairs move as sound waves come into the ear. The movements make signals go to your brain. Your brain uses the data for balance.

B. Now, rewrite the passage with your new vivid verbs. Add in precise nouns and active adjectives too.

_____

_____

_____

_____

_____

_____

_____

_____

_____

_____

_____

_____

_____

_____

To parents Ask your child to review one of their old pieces of writing and replace any dull verbs with more vivid ones.

Adverbs 1

> **Adverbs** tell more about verbs, adjectives and other adverbs. Many adverbs are formed by adding –*ly*. There are many different types of adverbs.
> - Adverbs of manner – tell us how something happens.
> - Adverbs of time – tell us when something happens.
> - Adverbs of frequency – tell us how often something happens.
> - Adverbs of purpose – tell us why something happens.
> - Adverbs of place – tell us where something happens.
> - Adverbs of degree – make the meaning stronger or weaker.

A. Here is a list of adverbs. Decide whether they are adverbs of manner (M), time (T), frequency (F), purpose (Pp), place (P) or degree (D).

A absolutely almost always	**B** because bitterly blissfully	**C** candidly certainly completely	**D** daily deliberately downstairs	**E** enough even ever	**F** fairly far fervently
G generously gleefully gracefully	**H** here highly home	**I** immediately inquisitively inward	**J** jaggedly jokingly joyously	**K** keenly kiddingly kind-heartedly	**L** lazily less lower
M miserably minutely monthly	**N** nearly nearby never next	**O** oddly offensively only outside	**P** parallel playfully purposely	**Q** quaintly quickly quite	**R** rapidly rather repeatedly

S seldom slightly somewhere	**T** terribly thoroughly too	**U** ultimately underground usually	**V** vastly verbally violently	**W** well while wholly	**Y** yearly yearningly yesterday **Z** zealously zestfully

B. Complete the following sentences with adverbs from the box.

deeply	eventually	critically	enigmatically
tonight	most	clearly	wrongly

1. It was clear that the couple were _____ in love from the way they looked into each other's eyes.

2. _____, after much persuasion, I took my mother's advice.

3. The accident left the victims _____ wounded and they had to undergo emergency surgery.

4. Mrs Thomas smiled _____ at her students and none of them knew what she was thinking about.

5. After a long day at work, we are going to have fun _____!

6. A healthy diet and exercise are the _____ effective ways to lose weight.

7. _____, Jaden had no excuse for his bad behavior and could not find anything to say.

8. Wilbur was _____ accused of stealing but there was no way to prove his innocence.

To parents Ask your child to choose 10 adverbs from the list in Part A and make sentences with them.

29

Adverbs 2

Adverbs answer questions like *how, when, where, how often, how many* or *how much.*

Vague: Should teachers allow calculators in math class?

Better: Should teachers <u>ever</u> allow calculators in math class?

A.   Use a complete sentence to fully answer each question as best as you can. Include an adverb from the box below in each answer.

| accurately | always | clearly | correctly | | daily | finally | ever |
| quickly | seldom | too | noticeably | | often | usually | never |

1.   How often do you use a calculator?

   _____

2.   Where do people carry calculators?

   _____

3.   In what ways could calculators cause problems?

   _____

4.   When do teachers encourage you to use a calculator?

   _____

5.   How much does a basic calculator cost?

   _____

6. At what type of store would you shop for a calculator?

_____

7. How many calculators should a classroom provide?

_____

8. What advantages do you see in using calculators?

_____

B. Complete the following table. Form the adverb from each adjective.

Adjective	Adverb	Adjective	Adverb
sad		simple	
frequent		hurried	
fatal		exasperated	
magical		defiant	
careful		boastful	

Complete the sentences using the adverbs in the table above.

1. The fervent admirer came by to see her _____.

2. The rebellious teenager spoke _____ to her mother.

3. Please walk _____ as the floor is wet.

4. The earthquake left many people _____ wounded.

To parents   Ask your child to write more sentences using the other adverbs from the table.

Adverbs 3

Adverbs can help describe how a person speaks or acts.

Okay: "It's my turn now," said Travis.

Better: "It's my turn now," said Travis boastfully.

A. Imagine that you are a movie director. Tell each actor how to say his or her line by writing an adverb after the verb.

HINT: Imagine coaxing the most believable performance out of each actor!

1. *[At a hospital]* "What did the doctor say?" asked Gina ___anxiously___.

2. *[In a traffic jam]* "How close are we?" said Haroun _____.

3. *[In a tent]* "I'm sitting on rocks and roots," complained Kate _____.

4. *[While skydiving]* "Whose bright idea was this?" thought Dan _____.

5. *[At a mall]* "I need a bigger allowance," stated LaNiqua _____.

6. *[In a blizzard]* "Come inside right now!" called Dad _____.

7. *[While dancing]* "Whoa! This is my favorite song!" Amy said _____.

8. *[Exercising]* "I can't keep this up forever!" called Lyndee _____.

B. Improve the following paragraphs with suitable adverbs to show how the speakers are speaking. Rewrite each paragraph.

1. "Stop that!" yelled Maggie, "I really hate it when people pull my hair!"

   "Oh come on Maggie," smirked Peter, "It was just for fun."

   "Leave her alone," ordered Mum.

_____

_____

_____

_____

_____

2.   "Over here," whispered Jean.

"Why did you drag me to this scary house?" asked Janet, all the while looking over her shoulder.

"Don't be such a coward," said Thomas, "You're such a baby."

"I'm not!" protested Janet, "Stop calling me that!"

_____

_____

_____

_____

_____

_____

_____

Add Adjectives and Adverbs

Adjectives usually go before the word they modify. Adverbs can go before or after the word they modify. You can add both kinds of words to improve a sentence.

Okay: Perry took his time getting ready.

Better: Perry always took his sweet time getting ready.

Perry defiantly took his sweet time getting ready.

A.   Rewrite each sentence about Perry. Add an adjective wherever it makes sense. Add an adverb before or after the word it modifies. Revise the sentence as needed.

HINT: Think of a useful detail. Then weave it in with an adverb.

1.   Perry's hobby is drawing landscapes.

_____

2.   He finds ideas near his house.

_____

3.   He observes in silence.

_____

4.   Perry blends colors in new ways.

_____

5.   Perry dreams of becoming an artist.

_____

B. Make the paragraph better by adding adjectives and adverbs where appropriate.

The warriors fought off the invaders. They had to rescue their leader as soon as possible. She was being held captive by their enemies. When they reached her cell, they saw that she had been hurt. There were bruises on her arms and legs and she could not move. They grabbed her and carried her away.

_____

_____

_____

_____

_____

_____

_____

_____

_____

_____

_____

To parents Ask your child to study a piece of artwork and write an elaborated paragraph on it.

35

Synonyms 1

Synonyms are words that mean the same, or nearly the same. Good writers use synonyms to express an idea in a more appealing or unexpected way.

Okay: This <u>news</u> may <u>worry</u> the senator's loyal <u>people</u>.

Better: This <u>rumor</u> may <u>jolt</u> the senator's loyal <u>followers</u>.

A.   Read the word at the top of each stack. List all the synonyms for it that you car

HINT: Act out each word in different ways to help you think of synonyms.

eat (verb)

suddenly (adverb)

mistake (noun)

fancy (adjective)

B. Complete the following sentences with synonyms of the words in brackets.

1. She was extremely _____ (lucky) to escape _____ (serious) injury.

2. The vehicle _____ (banged) into her while she was crossing the road.

3. Although she was not that _____ (badly) injured, she suffered some broken bones and temporary disability.

4. Still, she did not let her injuries _____ (depress) her.

5. She remains _____ (positive) and looks forward to _____ (new) experiences.

6. After her narrow escape, she decided to take a long _____ (holiday).

7. She traveled to many _____ (well-known) cities.

8. She enjoyed her _____ (travels) to various parts of the world.

9. She tried a variety of each country's _____ (dishes).

10. The strength of her character was _____ (admired) by many.

11. She also _____ (aided) those who were less fortunate than her.

12. She became a _____ (model) for many others.

Synonyms 2

Why use ordinary words when you can use **synonyms** that SIZZLE? An outstanding vocabulary is one of the marks of a great writer.

Okay: Tamara was <u>eager</u> to earn her doctorate before she turned forty.

Better: Tamara was <u>devoted</u> to earning her doctorate before she turned forty.

Rewrite the following paragraphs by replacing the underlined words with better synonyms. Use a thesaurus to help you.

1.   I was so <u>interested</u> in my thriller that I almost did not hear the strange <u>soft</u> sound. At first it <u>seemed</u> like a cough. Then I realised that it was the <u>crying</u> of a child. I <u>looked</u> all around me but could not see anyone crying. <u>Suddenly</u>, someone tugged at my T-shirt from behind. I jumped in <u>shock</u>.

   _____

   _____

   _____

   _____

   _____

2.   Artic <u>adventurer</u> Helen Thayer looked out at the <u>never-ending</u> white ice pack that lay <u>before</u> her. She was to spend the next four weeks on the ice, <u>travelling</u> to the Magnetic North Pole and back. She would go there on foot, <u>pulling</u> her supplies on a sled, with only her black husky Charlie, as a <u>partner</u>. Charlie would <u>warn</u> her if she were <u>unlucky</u> enough to encounter any polar bears—a serious <u>danger</u> in the Arctic.

_____

_____

_____

_____

_____

3. The boar was <u>large</u>, and its <u>pointed</u> tusks were the longest he had ever seen. The arrow hit it, making the powerful <u>animal</u> squeal. <u>Enraged</u>, the boar <u>hurtled</u> straight at Sir Aramis. His <u>frightened</u> horse reared back, <u>throwing</u> him to the ground. Sir Aramis <u>stumbled</u> to one knee and <u>readied</u> another arrow with his <u>skillful</u> fingers.

_____

_____

_____

_____

_____

_____

To parents Ask your child to pick any ten of the underlined words from the paragraphs and create a list of synonyms for each of them.

Antonyms

Antonyms are words that are opposite in meaning. *e.g. lively → dull*

Complete the antonym stacks.

Antonyms for PLEASANT	Antonyms for SUCCESS	Antonyms for COLD

Antonyms for HUMBLE	Antonyms for LAZY	Antonyms for HAPPY

Antonyms for SMALL	Antonyms for DEFEAT	Antonyms for QUIET

Antonyms for SLOW	Antonyms for DULL	Antonyms for TASTY

Alternate with Antonyms

Replace a word with an antonym to switch the meaning of a sentence.

They served us a <u>delicious</u> lunch → They served us a <u>tasteless</u> lunch.

A.   Read each phrase below. Think of an antonym to replace the underlined word. Rewrite the phrase to give an opposite (or nearly opposite) meaning.

HINT: Sometimes it helps first to think of a synonym—then think of its opposite.

1. in the <u>fiction</u> section	
2.	a surprising <u>defeat</u> for us
3. arranged to meet at <u>dusk</u>	
4. job as the <u>assistant</u>	
5. <u>repair</u> the sculpture	
6.	would never <u>permit</u> this activity
7.	<u>organize</u> the play area
8. a souvenir to <u>cherish</u>	
9. gave a <u>humble</u> speech	
10.	sat near the <u>talkative</u> student
11. wrote a <u>powerful</u> essay	
12.	sang a <u>mellow</u> song

B. Expand each phrase into a complete sentence. Change the underlined words to include a synonym and an antonym. For example, "job as the assistant" might become "Today, Emil begins his career as the manager."

1. gifts for my teachers

    _____

2. happy to be home

    _____

3. met a pleasant lady

    _____

4. thought about things carefully

    _____

5. added to the dish

    _____

6. organized activity for the young

    _____

7. answer to the question

    _____

8. a minor victory

    _____

C. Look at the paragraphs below. What antonyms can you think of that show opposite meanings to the underlined words?

Some people think of Jenny as a rather <u>dull</u> person. Although she is very <u>careful</u>, she always does things <u>slowly</u>. <u>A petite and quiet girl</u>, she is often <u>on the sidelines</u> and many people often <u>don't notice</u> that she's around. As a student, she has many <u>achievements</u> and does <u>well</u> in her studies. However, people think of her as a <u>cold and unapproachable person</u>. Only her close friends know that she is actually <u>a warm, humble and optimistic person who is simply shy</u>.

Use antonyms to replace some of the words in the underlined phrases. Rewrite the paragraph above to create a completely opposite character to the one described above.

_____

_____

_____

_____

_____

_____

_____

_____

Active Advertising

Advertising interests people in products or services. Successful ads often include catchy slogans that are easy to remember. Who remembers stale slogans or tired ads?

A. Here are some slogans that were rejected because they were dull and unmemorable. Write a new, improved slogan that you think might attract business. An example has been given.

HINT: Pretend you are making up a commercial to appeal to your friends.

 REJECTED SLOGAN    **NEW, IMPROVED SLOGAN**

1. **Dento-Paste** is good for your teeth!   *Treat your teeth to Dento-Paste!*

2. Get goodness with **Greg's Cereal**.

3. Be safe! Fix it at **Manny's Garage**!

4. **Gummo**: Flavor that lasts and lasts.

5. Clean your clothes with **Sudzi**.

6. **Snorum** Mattress = Good Sleep

> **Advertisements** try to convince people to make purchases. Besides catchy slogans, advertisements also highlight the good qualities of a product or service. It tells you about the benefits of purchasing that product or service in a very succinct way.

B. Choose a slogan from the previous page. What product or service is it? Jot down a few benefits or qualities of the product or service.

PRODUCT: _____

BENEFITS: _____

_____

QUALITIES: _____

_____

Now create your own advertisement for the product or service. Remember to talk about the good qualities of the product or service and include your slogan! You may also want to include an illustration.

To parents   Ask your child to look at advertisements and identify the slogans and benefits that advertisers use.

45

Supporting Details 1

An idea without support is vague. Even a sentence that's technically correct can be unclear. You can improve your writing by adding clear, vivid details to strengthen an idea.

Vague: Felicia disliked her sandwich.

Supported: Felicia disliked her sandwich because it had too much mayonnaise and onions in it.

A.   Look at the topic sentence below. Some details have been provided. Think of other details that might support the topic sentence. Use the questions provided.

TOPIC: Every person needs a good night's sleep.

SUPPORTING DETAILS:

- Allows the body to rest and heal itself
- Insufficient sleeps can lead to lower immunity
- Get sick less often
- _____

   (How would it affect your thinking?)

- _____

   (How would you feel if you didn't get enough sleep?)

- _____

   (How would you feel if you did get a good night's sleep?)

B.   Now use the topic sentence and the supporting points to write a short paragraph on the topic.

_____

_____

_____

_____

_____

_____

C.   Read the sentences. Together, they should tell a story. But too much is missing. Add supporting details to strengthen each idea. Be sure sentences work together as a single story.

HINT: Ask yourself what more YOU would want or need to know to get a better idea.

1.   The news came on as usual _____

_____

2.   I generally pay little attention _____

_____

3.   But that night I couldn't turn away _____

_____

4.   I asked my parents _____

_____

5.   They shared stories with me _____

_____

Supporting Details 2

Here are five kinds of supporting details you can add to strengthen an idea. Good writers pick and choose among them to create the best possible work.

Kind of detail	Effective when you want to
Sensory details	Bring a description to life; spark readers' imagination
Incidents	Support a point by offering a related story
Examples	Show how specific cases or uses support your idea
Facts	Provide definitions, data or statistics
Quotations	Add evidence by citing someone's words on the subject

A.   Give examples of each kind of supporting detail for the following situations.

1.   Sensory details
     (a market scene)   _____

                              _____

2.   Incidents
     (be careful when   _____
     crossing the
     road)   _____

3.   Examples
     (encourage   _____
     recycling)
                              _____

4.   Facts
     (conservation)   _____

                              _____

5. Quotations   _____
   (support the arts)   _____

B. Plan to convince a parent or teacher that you have a good idea. Maybe it's getting a pet or learning to play an instrument. Write the goal inside the rectangle. Use the web to gather supporting details for your idea.

HINT: Think of something you've really wanted to do or have happen.

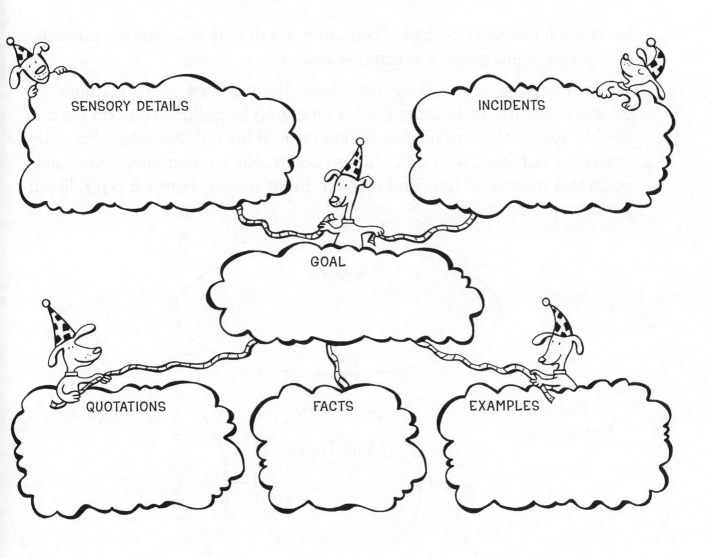

SENSORY DETAILS

INCIDENTS

GOAL

QUOTATIONS

FACTS

EXAMPLES

To parents Get your child to write a letter to a teacher to persuade that adult to consider the idea. Remind your child to include strong supporting details.

Supporting Details 3

Good writers build up on their main points by providing supporting details, facts and examples. This draws the readers into the stories by giving them more information.

A. Read the following passage. Then write the details in under the correct categories in the graphic organizer below.

The captain is a serious, unsmiling man. The wrinkles on his weather-beaten face hide acne scars from a time long forgotten. You can hardly see his eyes which are hidden by the brim of his hat. He wears his uniform crisp and starched, with an upturned collar. His commanding voice still inspires a mixture of fear and respect. In his mouth, hangs a pipe, like a permanent fixture.

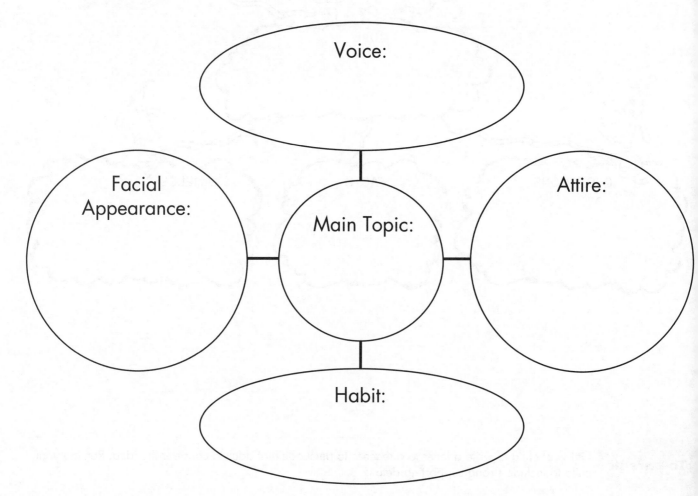

B. Expand the following topic sentence by providing supporting details. Then write out your paragraph in the space provided.

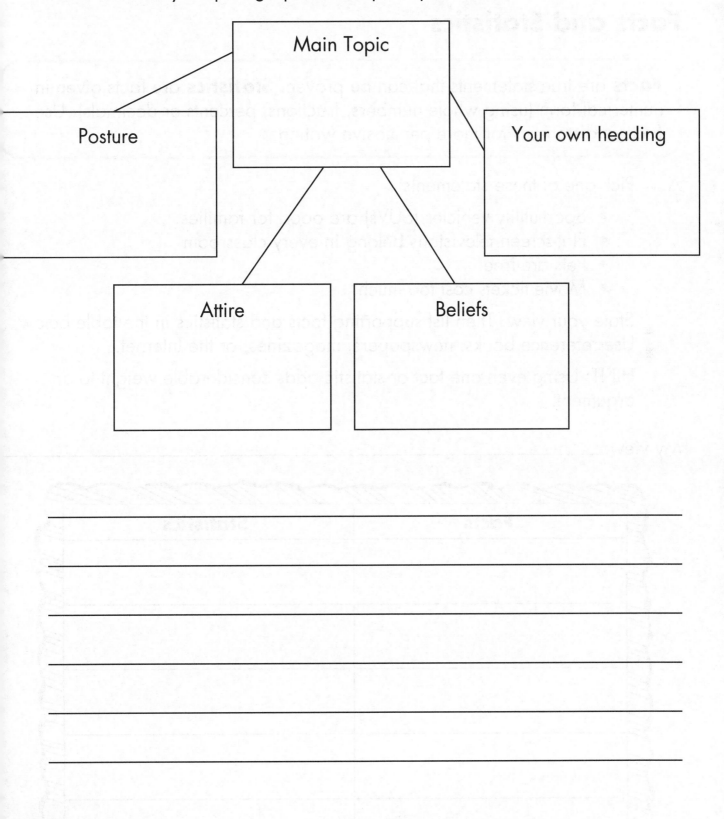

Main Topic

Posture

Your own heading

Attire

Beliefs

_____

_____

_____

_____

_____

_____

Facts and Statistics

Facts are true statements that can be proven. **Statistics** are facts given in numerical form (using whole numbers, fractions, percents or decimals). Use facts and statistics for more persuasive writing.

A. Pick one of these statements:

  • Sport-utility vehicles (SUVs) are good for families.
  • Flat-screen televisions belong in every classroom.
  • Pets are free.
  • Movie tickets cost too much.

State your view. Then list supporting facts and statistics in the table below. Use reference books, newspapers, magazines, or the Internet.

HINT: Using even one fact or statistic adds considerable weight to an argument.

My view: _____

Facts	Statistics

B. Plan and write a persuasive paragraph on your view, using the facts and statistics stated in Part A.

Beginning topic sentence	_____ _____ _____
Supporting facts and statistics	_____ _____ _____ _____ _____ _____ _____
Ending statement	_____ _____ _____ _____

Active Voice

We use active verbs when the subject in the sentence is the person or thing doing the action (the agent).

- <u>I</u> *ate* a late lunch.
- <u>You</u> *are being* unfair!
- <u>They</u> *will leave* for Japan next week.

In the above sentences, the subject and agent (*I, you* and *they* respectively) are doing the action (*ate, are being, will leave* respectively). Using the **active voice** keeps your sentences clear, direct, and more concise.

A. Underline the subject and rewrite the following sentences in the active voice.

1. Laughing and crying can only be done by one type of animal which is man.

   _____

2. The actors were cheered on by the appreciative audience.

   _____

3. Mr Johnson is held in high regard by everyone in the school.

   _____

4. Laughter is beginning to be taken seriously by hospital and health workers.

   _____

5. Much has been taught by the teachers since the beginning of the year.

   _____

B. Indicate with a tick (✔) the sentence that follows on the best. Think about whether the follow on sentence should focus on the subject or the object.

E.g. My school will be holding a big art exhibition.
(a) Many visitors will be attracted to it.
(b) It will attract many visitors. (✔)

1. The new neighbors are still constructing their house.
(a) The men and boys helped add a stable to the barn. ( )
(b) A stable to the barn was added by the men and boys. ( )

2. Mrs Lee wants to see Elvin and Andy during recess.
(a) She will punish them for not submitting their work. ( )
(b) They will be punished by her for not submitting their work. ( )

3. We have bought a new washing machine.
(a) It can do the washing much more effectively. ( )
(b) The washing can be done much more effectively. ( )

4. The terrible fire cost almost 30 lives and left scores injured.
(a) The local hospital is looking after them. ( )
(b) They are being treated in the local hospital. ( )

5. Ms Nair has finally completed her research.
(a) A scientific journal will publish her findings. ( )
(b) Her findings will be published in a scientific journal. ( )

6. Madonna was very popular in the 1980s.
(a) They played her songs on the radio every day. ( )
(b) Her songs were played on the radio every day. ( )

7. Damien is a very good artist.
(a) He won the first prize in this year's National Art Competition. ( )
(b) The first prize in this year's National Art Competition was won by him. ( )

8. Rice is very important in Asian cuisine.
(a) People eat it at almost every meal. ( )
(b) It is eaten at almost every meal. ( )

Passive Voice

We use passive verbs when the subject is NOT doing the action.
The **passive voice** is effective in these cases because it highlights the action and what is acted upon rather than the agent performing the action. The agent is mentioned only when it is important to the meaning of the sentence. The agent is <u>not mentioned</u> if:

- It does not add any new information. *e.g. He was arrested last night.*

- It is not important. *e.g. Our neighborhood is cleaned every day.*

- It is difficult to say who the agent is. *e.g. Many attempts have been made to find the Abominable Snowman.*

A. Rewrite the following sentences in the passive voice. Include the agent only if it is important to the meaning of the sentence.

1. Someone had broken into our neighbor's house while they were on holiday.

    _____

2. My boss has to sign the cheque.

    _____

3. The district judge offered Larnel a job as his chief adviser.

    _____

4. We needed to score a goal within the next two minutes.

    _____

5. People also knew Dr. Seuss as Theo Le Sieg.

    _____

B. Use the following words to write sentences in both the active and passive voice in the tenses given.

E.g. five people / see / the creature (Simple Past)
Write about five people: <u>Five people saw the creature.</u>
Write about the creature: <u>The creature was seen by five people.</u>

1. send / her luggage / to Perth / the airline / accidentally (Past Perfect)

   Write about the airline: _____.

   Write about her luggage: _____.

2. Jose / win / the spelling competition (Simple Past)

   Write about Jose: _____.

   Write about the spelling competition: _____.

3. a wild animal / attack / Karyn (Present Perfect)

   Write about a wild animal: _____.

   Write about Karyn: _____.

4. Mr and Mrs Chua / still / construct / their house (Present Continuous)

   Write about Mr and Mrs Chua: _____.

   Write about their house: _____.

5. One day / robots / do / all / our work (Future)

   Write about machines: _____.

   Write about our work: _____.

6. Martians / kidnap / my neighbors. (Present Perfect)

   Write about Martians: _____.

   Write about my neighbors: _____.

7. in Norway / English / speak / hardly (Simple Present)

   Write about Norwegians: _____.

   Write about English: _____.

Sensory Details Diagram

We perceive our environment through our senses: *hearing, smell, taste, touch* and *vision*. Add sensory details to your writing to help readers vividly summon ideas. Sensory details bring descriptions to life and help writers show, not just tell.

A.   Categorize the following details into the different types of details.

   1.   bright, glittery lights
   2.   constant chatter of people
   3.   salty and sweet air
   4.   dampness of the night air
   5.   smoky alleys
   6.   clanking of wares
   7.   a myriad of colors

TOPIC: The night market	
SIGHTS (*visual details*)	
SOUNDS (*auditory details*)	
SMELLS (*olfactory details*)	
TOUCH (*tactile details*)	
TASTES (*gustatory details*)	

Add other sensory details that you can think of to describe a night market.

B. Pick two different topics—places, things, events, or activities. Close your eyes and imagine each topic. List words, phrases, or ideas related to each sense in the charts.

HINT: Daydreaming is a good technique to use to lead you to new ideas!

TOPIC:	
SIGHTS (*visual details*)	
SOUNDS (*auditory details*)	
SMELLS (*olfactory details*)	
TOUCH/ TEXTURES (*tactile details*)	
TASTES (*gustatory details*)	

TOPIC:	
SIGHTS (*visual details*)	
SOUNDS (*auditory details*)	
SMELLS (*olfactory details*)	
TOUCH/TEXTURES (*tactile details*)	
TASTES (*gustatory details*)	

To parents Ask your child to pick one of the topics and write a paragraph about it with sensory details.

Incidents and Anecdotes

An **anecdote** is a short, entertaining story. It's about a particular event or incident that really happened. Anecdotes are often meant to be humorous or heartwarming.

A. Use the chart to list details for an anecdote about an actual incident in your life.
HINT: You might jot down ideas on scrap paper first, then organize them later.

The Incident _____

First...

Next...

Then...

The highlight was...

At last...

Looking back, I...

B. Use the details to write the anecdote. Make it amusing and entertaining for readers.

_____

_____

_____

_____

_____

_____

_____

_____

_____

_____

_____

_____

_____

To parents Remind your child that the anecdote should lead from one paragraph to another. Tell your child to use transition words to organize the essay in a logical way.

Actions Speak Louder

Have you ever read a boring book? You probably do not even want to bother reading till the end, right? To keep readers hooked to the story, it needs to have good **action**. Do not be too predictable when coming up with story actions. **The action builds on the problem**. Readers love action and secretly want something that makes them chuckle, cringe or be terrified. But how do you do this? **Put yourself in the story!**

Now have a go at creating your own story action, in about 4-5 sentences, for the following situations. Remember to put yourself in the story and make it as exciting as you can!

1. **Main Character:** An 11-year old boy named Fred
    Setting: A lonely park
    Problem: Fred finds a bag of money near a bin.

    _____

    _____

    _____

    _____

    _____

2. **Main Characters:** Two sisters named Anna and Jenna and their parents
    Setting: London
    Problem: Anna and Jenna can never get along. While on holiday with their parents in London, they have a terrible argument and Anna marches off on her own and soon gets lost in the crowd.

    _____

    _____

_____

_____

_____

3. **Main Characters:** Three friends named Marcus, Luke and Glenn
Setting: A coffee shop near their school
Problem: While having a drink at a nearby coffee shop after their soccer training, the three boys suddenly hear some shouting followed by screams.

_____

_____

_____

4. **Main Characters:** Eight-year-old Nick and his five-year-old brother Nigel
Setting: Home, early one Sunday morning
Problem: Nick's parents have told them to stay in bed and not come out of their room until 9am but both boys wake up by 7am and find nobody home.

_____

_____

_____

_____

Supporting Examples

One way to add detail is to give examples that support a main idea. **Supporting examples** can also refute or disprove an idea. Good examples help readers to make connections. Supporting examples often appear in nonfiction texts.

A. Support or refute each statement with an example. One has been done for you.

HINT: Examples vary in quality. Pick one that lends the most weight to your point.

1.	Our trip to Washington, D.C., made a lasting impression on me.	Visiting Ford's Theater, and seeing the actual seat where President Lincoln was shot, brought the drama of history alive to me for the first time.
2.	Having a pet can help children develop responsibility.	
3.	Rules in our school are not applied fairly to all students.	
4.	Many people do not get enough exercise to stay healthy.	
5.	Childhood is a carefree time of life.	
6.	People should behave quietly in public places.	

B. Think about the topic: Hobbies or Pastimes are Important. Then complete the table below.

Examples to Support	Examples to Refute

C. Use the points above to write a short paragraph about the statement.

_____

_____

_____

_____

_____

_____

_____

Details Diagram

You know that adding details often improves your writing. But what kinds of details should you add? There are many options. See the organizer below.

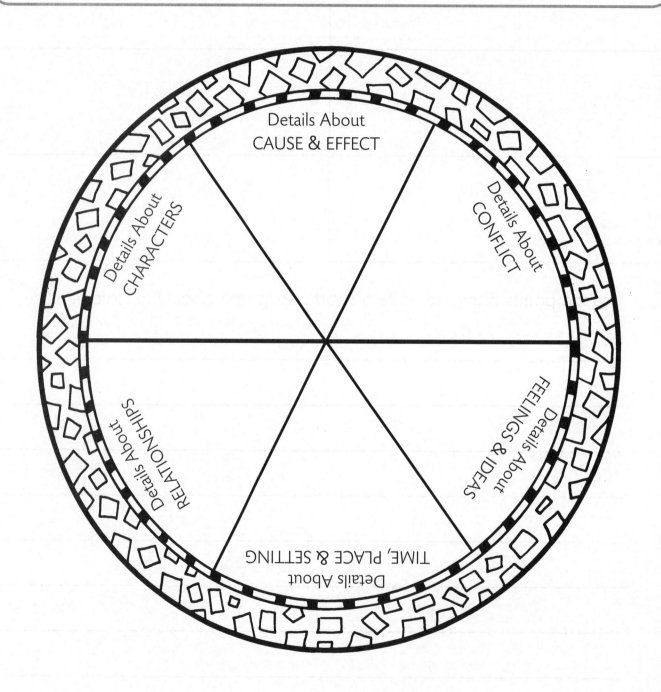

Now pick a topic for a story or essay. Using the organizer in the previous page think about additional details for your story or essay. Then write a short story or essay below.

_____

_____

_____

_____

_____

_____

_____

_____

_____

_____

Making a Choice

Many young writers often rush through the main event in a story and fail to develop the plot or action. One way to improve your writing is to include details. However, it is also important to include only relevant details that add to the action. You can amplify your writing by asking or answering the following questions:

- What did you do? (in slow motion!)
- What did you observe? (using the five senses)
- What did you think or feel? (emotionally and physically)
- What did you say?

A. Read the following paragraph. Use the details below to improve the original paragraph.

The motorcycle came speeding towards us. Suddenly, it tilted dangerously and crashed onto its side. The policemen came running out of their car and arrested the two injured robbers.

- Motorcyclists swerved as they came closer to the school gate
- Deafening crash
- The men trapped under the weight of the motorcycle
- I craned my neck to see if the riders survived

_____

_____

_____

_____

_____

B. Now add more details to the following scenarios.

While on a school camping trip in a jungle in Malaysia, I left my group to use the toilet. I stumbled upon an old hut and decided to investigate. I realized I had come across a drug den.

While on a school camping trip to a jungle in Malaysia – Describe the place you were camping at.

_____

_____

_____

I left my group to use the toilet – How did you feel while you left the group?

_____

_____

I stumbled upon an old hut – What might you have exclaimed or felt when you saw the hut?

_____

_____

I realized I had come across a drug den – How did you feel when you saw and realized it was a drug den?

_____

_____

To parents Get your child to include more details for the above paragraph.

Similes 1

A **simile** compares two things. Some similes compare two things using the word *like* or the structure *as* _____ *as*.

A. What can you compare the following objects / items to? What qualities do you associate with the objects / items? Brainstorm and complete the table below. The first one has been done for you.

	Main thing	Can be compared to...
1.	A fast car	A speeding bullet
2.	Identical twins	
3.	A clear sound	
4.	A sly person	
5.	A proud person	
6.	A wise person	

B. Use what you have written in the table above to complete the similes below.

1. The car was _____.

2. The twins were _____.

3. She heard a sound _____.

4. He was cunning and _____.

5. As she often succeeded in what she did, she became _____.

6. He was wise like _____.

C. The following are some common similes. Use them to complete the sentences.

as big as an elephant   as cold as ice   as quiet as a church mouse
as innocent as a lamb   as pure as snow   as thin as a rake
as slippery as an eel   as steady as a rock
as black as coal   as free as a bird

1. The giant was _____.

2. She was in such a foul mood that her face was _____.

3. The little girl is _____ and will believe anything you tell her.

4. That man cannot be trusted; he is _____.

5. The poor boy is _____ and looks like he has not eaten for weeks.

6. The shy and timid girl is _____ and seldom spoke to anyone.

7. Her stepmother is so unfeeling; she is _____.

8. The maiden had a heart of gold and she was _____.

9. Now that he no longer had any responsibilities, he felt

    _____.

10. You know that you can always count on Jason because he has always

    been _____.

Similes 2

A **simile** is a form of figurative language used to compare two things. Use similes to link things in fresh, imaginative ways. Similes usually use the word *like*, or the phrase *as* _____ *as.*

Ordinary statement: The scientist focused for hours.

Simile with like: The scientist focused <u>like a laser beam</u> for hours.

Simile with as: The scientist was <u>as focused as a microscope</u> for hours.

A.   Revise each statement by adding a simile. First try *like*. Then try *as* _____ *as.*

HINT: Visualize the idea to help you find ways to make better comparisons.

1.   Grandpa walks slowly. _____

_____

2.   We gaped at the double rainbow. _____

_____

3.   That old sofa is worn. _____

_____

4.   The foxes slip away. _____

_____

5.   She works hard every day. _____

_____

B. Choose a famous person you admire. Write two similes for each category.

Physical Appearance: _____

_____

Character: _____

_____

How the Person Moves: _____

_____

C. Now write a short description of the person. Use at least three of the similes that you have come up with.

_____

_____

_____

_____

_____

_____

To parents Ask your child to read a description and change some of the sentences to include similes.

73

Date: _____

Metaphors 1

A **metaphor** compares a subject to something else that seems unrelated. A metaphor gets readers to understand or experience one idea in terms of another in fresh or interesting ways.

Metaphor:　　　　　Zach is a fish all summer long.

Objects compared:　Zach = fish

Meaning conveyed:　Zach spends a lot of time swimming in the summer.

A.　Read each metaphor. Identify what is being compared by completing the equation. Then explain the meaning of the metaphor in your own words.

1.　That typewriter is a dinosaur.　　　_____ = _____

　　Meaning: _____

2.　My brother is a total couch potato.　_____ = _____

　　Meaning: _____

3.　Her home was a prison.　　　　　　_____ = _____

　　Meaning: _____

4.　It was a blanket of white outside.　　_____ = _____

　　Meaning: _____

5.　She went through a rollercoaster
　　of emotions.　　　　　　　　　　_____ = _____

　　Meaning: _____

B. Read each "plain" sentence below. Improve it by reworking it with a metaphor.

1. Trixie sleeps all day long. _____

_____

2. The cadets marched in the midday heat. _____

_____

3. Her salty tears fell as she read the letter. _____

_____

4. The hungry dog devoured his food. _____

_____

5. The stars lit up the midnight sky. _____

_____

C. Write a short poem or description of a storm. Include metaphors.

_____

_____

_____

_____

To parents Ask your child to think of metaphors to describe a memorable moment.

75

Metaphors 2

> **Metaphors** associate two concepts that normally would not be connected by stating or implying that one concept is the other. They help the writer to create a *visual picture* in the reader's mind.

A. Read each metaphor. Explain the meaning of the metaphor in your own words.

1. The defender was a rock.

   _____

2. The passengers were sardines in a can.

   _____

3. The truth immediately gushed out of his mouth.

   _____

4. My father's trust in me would be shattered.

   _____

5. They dug up the truth about the matter.

   _____

6. Her fury was a raging inferno, incinerating everything in its path.

   _____

B. Choose any object that you like. Describe this object as creatively as you can. What characteristics does it have? What does it do? How does it feel? How do you feel holding it? Does it have a smell or taste?

_____

_____

_____

_____

_____

C. What other things or concepts share similar qualities with your object? Try to be adventurous – the less obvious your association, the more interesting your metaphor will be. Can your object be an animal, a toy, a tool, a mode of transport or a person? Be as creative as possible! List at least six different things that it could be.

1. _____

2. _____

3. _____

4. _____

5. _____

6. _____

To parents   Repeat this exercise with your child for a person or place instead of an object.

Alliteration Headlines

Alliteration is the repetition of the same beginning consonant sound in a phrase. You can use alliteration to enhance the mood or meaning of creative writing.

No alliteration: the odor of the sauce cooking

Alliteration: the <u>s</u>weet-<u>s</u>cented, <u>s</u>immering <u>s</u>auce

A.   Think of adjectives that start with the same sound as each object.

1.   Friend   _____

2.   Bees   _____

3.   Sisters   _____

B.   Now, think of verbs that start with the same sound as each object.

1.   Friend   _____

2.   Bees   _____

3.   Sisters   _____

C.   Now, think of adverbs that start with the same sound as each object.

1.   Friend   _____

2.   Bees   _____

3.   Sisters   _____

D. Combine the adjectives, verbs and adverbs to write alliterative phrases for each object.

1. Friend _____

2. Bees _____

3. Sisters _____

E. Use each word in a three- to six-word headline. Start all words with the same consonant sound. Have some fun! The first one has been done as an example.

HINT: Think of clever headlines you've seen in newspapers and magazines.

1. baker   *Busy Baker Burns Buttermilk Biscuits*

2. pollution _____

3. harmful _____

4. money _____

5. doctor _____

6. champion _____

7. frozen _____

8. songs _____

Onomatopoeia 1

Some words can be used to describe sounds exactly as they sound. The use of such words is called **onomatopoeia** (on-oh-mat-uh-pee-uh). Onomatopoeic words are popular in comic books and graphic novels. They also capture your readers' attention because they make your story livelier. Here are some examples: *ah-choo, buzz, bang, boom, crunch, drip, ker-plonk, pow, rustle, zap.*

A. For each of the following situations, write a sentence with a suitable onomatopoeic word from the list provided.

> Huff-puff   Mmmm   Oops   Rip   Whack

E.g. You finally understood something that you had been confused about. Aha! The answers were suddenly as clear as day!

1. The curry your mum cooked for you was very delicious.

    _____

2. Your lift stopped working and you had to climb the stairs up to your flat on the thirteenth floor.

    _____

3. You dropped your worksheets all over the floor.

    _____

4. You tore your favorite pair of pants when you bent down to pick something up.

    _____

5. You missed giving your friend a high-five and accidentally hit his face instead.

_____

3. Now revise each of the following story beginnings. Use onomatopoeia to draw the reader into the setting or action. Write one or two sentences.

Example: *One rainy day, I walked to the hawker center near my house.*

Revision: *Splish! Splosh! My slippers splashed through the puddles as I ran for the hawker center.*

1. One Monday morning, Father was driving his van on a busy highway.

What might Father hear on the highway?

Revision: _____

_____

_____

_____

2. It was my school's annual sports day and I was running in the 100m race.

What sounds might you hear at the stadium?

Revision: _____

_____

_____

_____

To parents Ask your child to create a list of onomatopoeic words by looking up comic books or cartoons.

Date: _____

Onomatopoeia 2

Onomatopoeic words are popular with poets, entertainers and storytellers. They can be fun and lively to use. There may be no better word for a certain situation than using a word that sounds like what it means. For example:

The bacon <u>sizzled</u> in the pan.

A. Complete each sentence with an onomatopoeic word from the box.

pow	chatter	plopped	screeched	crackled
moo	popped	whack	splat	boom

1. _____! That punch landed squarely in his face.

2. The cork _____ when I pushed it out.

3. _____ went the whip on the wooden board.

4. The cows _____ calmly at one another.

5. The egg went _____ when I dropped it on the floor.

6. There was a loud _____ when the bomb exploded.

7. My teeth _____ whenever it gets too cold.

8. The jelly _____ onto the table.

9. The car _____ to a sudden halt.

10. The fire _____ as we gathered around it.

B. Choose eight onomatopoeic words from the cuckoo clock.
Use each in an entertaining sentence.
HINT: "Listen" for sounds to think of onomatopoeic words related to them.

1. _____

_____

2. _____

_____

3. _____

_____

4. _____

_____

5. _____

_____

6. _____

_____

7. _____

_____

8. _____

_____

bang boom

clang crackle

crunch drip

fizz grunt

hiss murmur

ooze puff

rattle

splat thud

whoosh

To parents Ask your child to look at some comics or children's stories to see how authors use onomatopoeia.

Idioms 1

An **idiom** is an expression whose meaning does not match the literal meaning of its words. If someone is *sitting on the fence*, the person is not really sitting on top of the fence. The idiom means that a person cannot make a decision about something.

A.   Below are some common idioms. Match each idiom with its meaning. Write the letter on the line.

> A.   by any means possible
> B.   to give up
> C.   to change for the better
> D.   to get over a stage of initial awkwardness
> E.   futile search
> F.   to behave unfairly
> G.   to try and improve
> H.   suffer the consequences of what one has done

1.   Turn over a new leaf _____

2.   Pull up one's socks _____

3.   Wild goose chase _____

4.   Hit below the belt _____

5.   Break the ice _____

6.   Throw in the towel _____

7.   Burn one's fingers _____

8.   By hook or by crook _____

B. Write the meaning of each idiom in your own words.
    HINT: Idioms can confuse readers who speak other languages than you
    do. Use with care!

1. see eye to eye   _____

2. spill the beans   _____

3. walk on thin ice   _____

4. feel blue   _____

5. no bed of roses   _____

6. backseat driver   _____

7. burn the midnight oil   _____

8. cut corners   _____

9. in hot water   _____

10. a blessing in disguise _____

Idioms 2

Idioms are phrases or expressions that have a *figurative* meaning. They cannot be taken literally and therefore, they are unique to a particular language. Take a look at some idioms and **idiomatic phrases** and their meanings in the box.

Idiom	Meaning
Kick the bucket	to die
Let the cat out of the bag	reveal a secret
Have a riot	enjoy oneself and have a good time
Get on like a house on fire	have a very good and close relationship
Sail close to the wind	take risks
A fish out of water	someone who is in an unfamiliar situation
Being in seventh heaven	being extremely happy
Smoking gun	definite proof of someone's guilt

A.   Choose from the list provided, the idiom that best completes each sentence.

> Long in the tooth
> Necessity is the mother of invention
> On the same wavelength
> Play devil's advocate
> Rome was not built in a day
> On a fool's errand

1.   The group worked well together and finished their project quickly as they were all _____.

2. Trying to _____, Maeve asked her team, "But what if Ruben is correct? Perhaps we should think about his proposal."

3. Old Mr Rosen had a tough time getting a job as most bosses thought he was a little _____ to be working as a salesman.

4. You must know that _____. It takes patience and good judgment to build a successful business.

5. Unable to afford expensive costumes, the dancers created their own costumes, proving that _____.

6. Poor Cathy knew that she was _____ when she tidied her house. Her children would mess it up again in minutes.

B. For each of the following idioms, explain its meaning and write a sentence using the idiom appropriately.

1. When pigs fly – _____

_____

2. Let sleeping dogs lie – _____

_____

3. Over my dead body – _____

_____

To parents Ask your child to use some of the idioms on the previous pages in sentences.

87

Collocations

A **collocation** is two or more words that often go together. These word combinations just sound 'right' to English speakers, who use them all the time. On the other hand, other combinations may be unnatural and just sound 'wrong'. Having the right word collocations will make your writing sound more natural and easily understood.

A. Circle the best answer for each of the following sentences.

1. We need to conduct a _____ investigation before we inform the staff.
    (1) complete   (2) thorough   (3) meticulous

2. I could not finish my test because I had run _____ time.
    (1) out of   (2) through   (3) over

3. _____ by, you will feel better about your loss.
    (1) As time goes   (2) When the time comes   (3) In time

4. Thomas left his job _____ the grounds of unfair treatment.
    (1) at   (2) in   (3) on

5. Gordon was confused as to why his friends were _____ ignoring him.
    (1) unashamedly   (2) blatantly   (3) plainly

6. Due to the deep _____ between the two brothers, they never attend any family events together.
    (1) animosity   (2) brotherhood   (3) loathing

7. My son is so camera-_____ that he hides whenever someone tries to take a photo of him.
    (1) coy   (2) shy   (3) wary

8. The student escaped being punished because of a serious _____ in judgment on the part of his teacher.
    (1) lapse   (2) slip   (3) failure

9. When Mr Reggie listens to old songs, they remind him of a _____ era.
    (1) past   (2) olden   (3) bygone

10. Nobody suspected that he had a _____ agenda behind his smiling, innocent facade.
    (1) veiled   (2) hidden   (3) secret

B. Fill in the blanks with the correct word to complete the collocation. The meaning of the collocation is provided in the bracket.

carpet	jump	dime	ovation
lend	hand	world	regard
price	whim		

1. During our recent trip to China, we got the red- _____ treatment wherever we went. *(special treatment)*

2. At the recent IT Fair, digital cameras were being sold for a _____. *(very cheaply)*

3. Do not _____ to conclusions before finding out what really happened. *(prejudge)*

4. Mr Powell received a standing _____ from the audience at the end of his inspiring speech. *(applause)*

5. Sarah is very frugal and almost never buys things on _____. *(suddenly)*

6. I hope you can _____ me a _____ and clean my room for me today. I need to get some urgent work done. *(help)*

7. Tamara's pets mean the _____ to her and she will do anything for them. *(very important)*

8. Helen is now paying the _____ for her laziness. She failed her last exam terribly. *(be punished)*

To parents Ask your child to check the meaning of the following collocations and use them in sentences: *fever pitch, filthy rich, setting the record straight, behind bars*

Exaggerate to Elaborate

When you exaggerate, you stretch the truth. **Exaggeration** makes things seem much bigger or smaller. It can make things seem much better or worse.

Okay: Kenny was very hungry.

Better: Kenny was so hungry he could eat a horse.

A.   Read each description. How is each description an exaggeration? Write down the point you think each sentence was trying to make.

1.   She must have a brain the size of a pea!

   _____

2.   I bet this car can go faster than the speed of light.

   _____

3.   I have a million things to do and so little time to do them.

   _____

4.   I could smell that pungent odor a mile away!

   _____

5.   My back is really killing me.

   _____

6.   Why does it take her forever to get ready?

   _____

7.   He worships the ground she walks on and would move mountains for her.

   _____

B. Make each sentence better by adding some exaggeration. It is fine to be funny!
HINT: Think of how tall tales, folk songs, and jokes use exaggeration.

1. The coat was too long.

_____

2. She parked far from the store.

_____

3. Our dog snores loudly.

_____

4. Maria was thirsty.

_____

5. We waited for a moment.

_____

6. The movie was long.

_____

7. I burned our dinner.

_____

8. Why do people like to fish?

_____

Dialogue Details

A **dialogue** is a conversation between people. In writing, dialogue refers to the words people say. You read dialogue in stories, articles, scripts and plays.

A. Read the following conversation. Then continue the dialogue. You can add in additional characters if you wish. Remember to add in the correct punctuation marks.

"Why is Mandy taking such a long time to get here? Didn't you say that she was on her way?" asked Caroline.

"Well, that's what she told me!" protested Jim.

"Do think something might have happened to her?"

"Oh look! There she is!"

"What took you so long?" asked Caroline.

"I'm sorry," said Mandy, "Something happened at home."

_____

_____

_____

_____

_____

_____

_____

B. Use this form to write a dialogue about a disagreement between yourself and another character. Write the other person's name on each blank line. Then write what each person says.

HINT: Read your dialogue aloud. Does it sound like actual speech? If not, revise it.

YOU:	
_____:	
YOU:	
_____:	
YOU:	
_____:	
YOU:	
_____:	
YOU:	
_____:	

Getting Ideas

Sometimes you are required to write to a prompt which can be anything from a subject to a topic to a story-starter. These prompts are designed to get your creative juices flowing. However, to make your story unique, you need to do some brainstorming and come up with some fun ideas.

A.   Twist the ending of the following synopsis from the one provided.

You find your classmate crying at a corner during recess one day. You learn that she was being bullied by the class bully. You decide to teach the bully a lesson.

Funny Ending:

Knowing that the bully has a secret fear of spiders, you place a spider covertly into his pencil case. When the bully sees it, he screams like a girl and ends up embarrassing himself in front of everyone.

Tragic Ending:

_____

_____

_____

_____

_____

_____

_____

_____

B.	The following is a plot of a famous movie. Re-imagine the story in a different genre.

Movie: Harry Potter and the Sorcerer's Stone
Genre: Adventure/Fantasy
Plot:
On his 11th birthday, Harry Potter receives extraordinary news from a giant named Hagrid that he is a wizard. He travels to Hogwarts School of Witchcraft and Wizardry to learn the trade of being a wizard. Here, he meets his two best friends, Ron Weasley, an expert at Wizard Chess but not very brave, and Hermione Granger, a girl with non-magic parents but super-smart. However, trouble brews at Hogwarts as Harry suspects some-one is planning to steal the sorcerer's stone.

New Genre: Comedy
Your Plot:

_____

_____

_____

_____

_____

_____

_____

_____

_____

_____

To parents Get your child to randomly select five words. Set a timer for 20 minutes and simply free write, incorporating these five words.

95

Character Planner

> Making your characters memorable is important to getting your reader to empathize or be interested in the character.

A. Think about a story you might write. Make up traits for each character. Use the following chart to name and plan each character. Include words, phrases, anecdotes or other details to help the readers get to know each one.

MAIN MALE CHARACTER

Name	
Personality	
Appearance	
Other details	

MAIN FEMALE CHARACTER

Name	
Personality	
Appearance	
Other details	

HELPER OR ADVICE GIVER

Name	
Personality	
Appearance	
Other details	

VILLAIN OR TROUBLEMAKER

Name	
Personality	
Appearance	
Other details	

B. Choose one of the characters above and write a paragraph about the character.

_____

_____

_____

_____

Setting the Scene

A good description of the setting creates a rich image and enhances the mood for the reader. A poor description leaves the reader struggling for a mental image and disconnects him from the characters and action. One way to describe the setting clearly is by using sensory information to help the reader experience the story.

A. Add on to the following scenario and create a setting for it. You may use the words provided to help you and add your own sensory information.

Annie walked into the <u>bakery</u>, searching for something to appease her hunger.

Sights:
Buns, doughnuts, muffins, cookies, trays with crumbs on them, stainless steel counters, bagels, fresh bread

Sounds:
cash register, oven timers going off, customer conversations, the clicking of plastic tongs for selecting the confections

Smells:
yeasty dough, sugar, melted butter, crusty bread, toasted bread, roasted nuts, maple or honey, spices, browning cheeses

Tastes:
fresh bread, spices, yeast, sugary glazes, nuts, grains, seeds, chocolate, coffee, water, jams, honey, butter, cream cheese, fudge cakes

Touch:
sticky buns, licking fingers, warm rolls, ripping crusty bread apart, light crispy layers of puff pastry, chewy bread, butter oozing onto fingertips

_____

_____

_____

_____

_____

_____

_____

_____

_____

_____

_____

_____

_____

_____

_____

_____

To parents Get your child to come up with sensory information for a birthday party.

Plotting

A good **plot** keeps the reader hooked. It is what the story is about. Writers often use techniques such as **suspense** and **foreshadowing**. Suspense keeps the reader wanting to find out what happens next while foreshadowing hints at what is going to happen next. For example: *"Sarah's heart beat wildly as she blinked at the threat written on the dirty piece of paper…"* This is an example of foreshadowing as it hints at trouble for the character.

For each of the following conflicts write the sequence of events. Make sure that there is a climax in the plot and a resolution.

1. Jamie, a new student, tops her class in the English exam, making the most popular and smartest girl in the class very envious.

    Event 1: _____

    _____

    _____

    Event 2: _____

    _____

    _____

    Climax: _____

    _____

    _____

Resolution: _____

_____

_____

2. No matter how hard Sasha's swimming coach encourages her, she still feels she's not good enough to compete at the national level.

Event 1: _____

_____

_____

Event 2: _____

_____

_____

Climax: _____

_____

_____

Resolution: _____

_____

_____

Build a Story

Planning your writing is a very important first step. A **Story Hand** can be useful and it's easy to follow:

- The palm of the hand contains the <u>setting</u> and <u>characters</u>.
- The thumb is the <u>grabber</u> and a good beginning is important to grab the reader's attention.
- The pointer finger is the <u>conflict</u>.
- The middle finger is the <u>action of the story</u>.
- The ring finger is the <u>climax</u>.
- The little finger is the <u>resolution</u>.

Now try creating a story map based on the Story Hand for the prompts below.

Something very precious to you goes missing...

- Characters (Who?)

_____

_____

_____

- Setting (Where? When?)

_____

_____

_____

- Grabber (What?)

_____

_____

_____

- Problem or Challenge (What?)

_____

_____

_____

- Events (What happens?)

_____

_____

_____

- Climax (What happens?)

_____

_____

_____

- Resolution (What? How?)

_____

_____

_____

To parents Ask your child to pick a story they like and break up the plot into its components.

My Autobiography

An **autobiography** is an account of a person's life written by that person. It spans the entire life of the author, from childhood to adulthood where the author recounts his experiences and feelings. When writing an autobiography, it helps to think of particular events that made an impact on your life.

Write your own autobiography. Here are a few prompts to help write the autobiography of your choice.

- What is your fondest memory of your childhood?
- Who are the people who made an impact on you when you were young and in what way did they influence you?
- What events shaped your life and what happened?
- Describe your teachers throughout your primary school.
- Describe the most difficult thing you have had to do in your life.

Here is a graphic organizer that you can use to plan and write your autobiography.

MY AUTOBIOGRAPHY

Setting:

_____

Time frame:

_____

People who had an impact on me:

_____

_____

_____

Events that had an impact on me:

_____

_____

_____

_____

What I learned or how this event/experience changed me:

_____

_____

_____

_____

To parents Ask your child to keep a journal for a week then compile the entries into a short autobiography.

105

Biographical Sketch

Biographies, like autobiographies, are also the true accounts of a person's life. However, in biographies, someone else writes about the main character whereas in autobiographies, the main character of the life story is the same person who is telling the story.

A. Read the following excerpts and indicate if it is a biography or an autobiography.

"Do you think she'll do it?" Tanya asked Peter.
"I think so. She seems very determined this time," Peter responded.
I was surprised to hear of Peter's pretty accurate observation. Yes, this time I was hell-bent on clearing the contents of my desk which resembled a mini Mount Everest.

Autobiography / Biography

Nobody in the office had seen Michelle neaten her work station. Not once in the five years that she had been working for the company. In fact, she had always seemed a little too smug about her 'organized mess' as she liked to call it.

Autobiography / Biography

Dr. Seuss is indeed an inspiration for young writers. Despite being rejected twenty-seven times before his first children's book, *"And To Think That I Saw It on Mulberry Street"* got published, and despite being written off by his high-school art teacher, Dr. Seuss, born Theodor Seuss Geisel, never gave up.

Autobiography / Biography

Twenty-seven publishers have rejected it. "Theodor, you'll never be a real artist!" Her words still flash across my mind during moments like this. Nevertheless, I will not be discouraged. My book will be published, somehow.

Autobiography / Biography

B. Fill in the following graphic organizer with details of a famous person (dead or still alive). Then write out a short biography of this person.

Name:

Background and early life (include date and place of birth and information about family):	Characteristics:
Major accomplishments:	How these accomplishments changed the world:

What you admire about this person:

Select a Sentence

A.   Use this table to help you create original sentences. Pick a word or phrase from each column. Add details to weave them together into an interesting sentence. See the example below.

HINT: Arrange the sentence parts in any order that makes sense.

When?	Who/What?	Did What?	Where?	How?
after lunch	two horses	appeared	in the tunnel	easily
before dawn	a message	came forward	behind the house	fearlessly
during art	my neighbor	exploded	below the surface	foolishly
earlier	a package	raced	on a bus	in silence
last night	a siren	shrieked	over the hill	lovingly
on Tuesday	her sister	snuck	through the gate	modestly
yesterday	that stranger	warned	under the porch	with humor

1.   <u>On Tuesday, the two horses fearlessly raced through the gate to reach shelter.</u>

2.   _____

_____

3.   _____

_____

4.   _____

_____

5.   _____

_____

B. Pick one sentence you wrote and expand it into a story.

_____

_____

_____

_____

_____

_____

_____

_____

_____

_____

_____

To parents Ask your child to find ways of improving the story.

Vary Sentence Types

A **declarative** sentence 'declares' or states. It is the most common kind of sentence. It ends with '.'
An **interrogative** sentence 'asks'. It ends with '?'
An **exclamatory** sentence 'exclaims' or 'cries out'. It conveys feelings. It ends with '!'
An **imperative** sentence 'commands' or 'requests'. It ends with '.' The subject is 'you', even if unwritten.

A.   Identify each sentence by its type.

1.   Maria Tallchief was a Native American dancer. _____

2.   Have you ever heard of her? _____

3.   How famous she was in her time! _____

4.   Look her up in an encyclopedia. _____

5.   Did you know she was born in Oklahoma? _____

6.   I totally adore ballet! _____

B.   Write...

1.   an *interrogative* sentence about Beijing.

_____

2.   a *declarative* sentence about dance.

_____

3.   an *exclamatory* sentence about a celebrity.

_____

4.   an *imperative* sentence about proper behavior at a concert.

_____

C.   For each of the following scenarios, write a short paragraph. Include at least one of each type of sentence in your paragraph.

1.   Write a paragraph about your own country.

_____

_____

_____

_____

2.   Write a paragraph about a famous personality.

_____

_____

_____

_____

_____

_____

To parents   Ask your child to pick a topic above and write an additional paragraph on it.

Vary Sentence Length

Good writers vary the lengths of their sentences to keep the reader interested and control the pace of their stories. Long sentences allow lots of ideas to be included but having too many long sentences can make your writing too tiring to read. Too many short sentences can make your writing choppy and awkward.

A. The following passages are made up of sentences of similar lengths. Rewrite the passages using long and short sentences.

Example:

When my family visited Nepal last year, we were on the lookout for some native Nepalese art. In Kathmandu, we found many beautiful statues and intricately woven wall hangings. However, we could not find anyone selling paintings by a particular painter that my mother had seen somewhere before. We were very disappointed when we left Kathmandu, empty-handed.

When my family visited Nepal last year, we were on the lookout for some native Nepalese art such as statues and woven wall hangings. Kathmandu stores had many beautiful statues and intricately woven wall hangings. However, we were disappointed that paintings by a particular painter that my mother wanted were difficult to find. Sadly, we left Nepal empty-handed.

1. *After what seemed like ages, Timothy came round. Gerald heaved a sigh of relief. He was petrified when Timothy had fainted. His other friend Jason was in a panic too. They did not know what to do. Gerald had tried calling Timothy's mother but to no avail. There was nobody else around in that deserted field.*

_____

_____

_____

_____

2. I was thrown onto the floor of the train as it jerked and came to a halt. Many other passengers were also thrown off-balance, falling on top of one another like falling dominoes. The pudgy man standing behind me was now almost on me, his massive bulk nearly squashing the air out of me. Just as I managed to squirm my way to freedom, the lights in the train flickered and finally went out.

_____

_____

_____

_____

B. Write a paragraph for the following scenario. Create suspense and make the reader feel excited.

You are in a dream. In the first part of your dream you are being chased through a forest by a pack of rabid dogs.

_____

_____

_____

_____

_____

_____

To parents Read excerpts from children's books with your child and point out how the author uses a variety of sentence lengths to create a certain effect.

Making a List

> Writing is not just about stories or compositions. Lists are a fun, quick and authentic way to enjoy writing. We call writing a list purposeful writing as it helps you to achieve something. For example, doing up a To-Do list helps you to prioritize and focus on the tasks that you need to complete.

A. Research has proven that children's TV programs are not really beneficial to children in any way. Create four reasons to refute this.

Top 4 Reasons Why Children's TV Shows Can Be Good for Them

1. _____

2. _____

3. _____

4. _____

B. Your younger sibling is starting school soon. Write a list of six things he / she can look forward to on the first day of school.

Top 6 Things to Look Forward to on Your First Day at School

1. _____

2. _____

3. _____

4. _____

5. _____

6. _____

C. If you had to worry about nothing and nobody stood in your way, what would you do with your life? Think of five items.

My Wish List for My Life

1. _____

2. _____

3. _____

4. _____

5. _____

D. You are planning a surprise birthday party for your mother. List down the items you will need to prepare for the party.

Mum's Surprise Party Plan

1. _____

2. _____

3. _____

4. _____

5. _____

6. _____

7. _____

8. _____

How Things Work

An **explanation composition** or **'how-to' composition** tells us how something works or why something happens. It is written in the second person and the present tense. Conjunctions such as *although, however, furthermore* are usually used to link the detail sentences.

A.   Look at the following title. Topic sentences have been provided for each paragraph. Provide supporting details and use conjunctions to develop paragraphs. Use the organizer below to guide you.

Introduction: a very general sentence that sets up the topic sentence

↓

Topic Sentence: states the main point and lets readers know what the paragraph is about

↓

Support with details – in order of importance

| How and why something begins? | → | What happens next? | → | What happens after? | → | What happens in the end? |

Conclusion: A summary sentence that reminds the reader of the most important message in the composition

Title: How You Can Be a Sprinter

On your marks. Get set. Go!

_____

_____

Running on your toes improves your speed.

_____

_____

_____

_____

Lifting your knees higher helps too.

_____

_____

_____

Propel yourself with your arms.

_____

_____

_____

Relaxing your head helps your whole body.

_____

_____

_____

Cut the Clutter

It is important to write clearly and concisely. Getting to the point quickly makes your writing easier to read. Cut out the clutter by:

- cutting out words that express the same idea

  Redundant: <u>The reason</u> I was tired was <u>because</u> I had worked for six <u>straight</u> hours <u>without stopping</u>.

  Better: I was tired because I had worked for six straight hours.

- removing unnecessary words that have no use

  Redundant: I drank half <u>of</u> the coffee before I started feeling sick.

  Better: I drank half the coffee before I started feeling sick.

- cutting out unnecessary adverbs or adjectives *eg. really, basically, actually, probably, extremely, very, etc.*

  Redundant: I was <u>actually</u> so upset with Tina that I <u>basically</u> screamed my head off at her.

  Better: I was so upset with Tina that I screamed my head off at her.

A. Make the following sentences more concise by replacing the underlined redundant words. Make sure the meaning of the sentence remains the same.

1. Marianne has managed to lose all excess weight by dieting <u>as well as</u> exercising most days of the week.

   _____

   _____

2. <u>In the event that</u> your pet falls terribly sick, <u>it is of utmost importance</u> that you take it to a vet <u>as soon as possible</u>.

   _____

   _____

3. <u>The fact that</u> I have to wake up <u>early in the morning</u> at 5.30am <u>sharp</u> <u>in order to</u> make it to school <u>exactly</u> on time combined <u>together</u> with the <u>nearly</u> three hours I take to commute <u>back and forth from home and school</u> make me <u>extremely</u> exhausted every <u>single</u> day.

_____

_____

B. Revise the following passage by cutting the clutter.

At that point in time, I was just a mere five years old in age. Many claim that it is an age where children become fascinated with nearly everything they see and it was with the best of intentions that my mother took me to the zoo almost each and every week. I am of the opinion that my mother did that to inculcate in me an undying and everlasting love of nature and animals as the end result of our early weekly zoo trips.

Looking back in retrospect, I realize that the seeds of my mother's confusion in all matters pertaining to me had already begun to be sown then. She never came to realize that the love of the outdoors would never be planted in me. I hated the heat of the sun, burning down my back. And I truly and absolutely hated the reeking stench of the animals that viciously assaulted my senses.

_____

_____

_____

_____

_____

_____

_____

To parents Look through a recent piece of writing with your child and revise it by cutting out redundancies.

Elaborating Without Repeating

Sometimes writers repeat their points when adding details by saying the same thing in a different way. This can make the writing dull and tedious to read. It is important to provide details while keeping your writing succinct.

Repetitious: I was too afraid to run and my fear kept me rooted to the spot. All I wanted to do was dig a hole and hide in it.

Better: My fear kept me rooted to the spot. All I wanted to do was bury myself in a hole so deep no one would ever find me.

A. Rewrite the following description. Remove the repetitious information or phrases and add other details to the description.

Michael sank into his chair in despair. What had he done? He knew that he wanted to get back at the people who hurt him. He wanted them to experience the hurt he went through and the suffering that he endured. They had to pay for the pain they caused him. What he did not expect was that his actions would end up hurting the people closest to him as well.

_____

_____

_____

_____

_____

_____

_____

B. Elaborate on the following sentences. Remember to keep your writing succinct. Add new details to your description instead of repeating the ones you wrote.

Before I realized it, the monkey had escaped from its enclosure and was running through the zoo.

the monkey – Describe the monkey and its movement.

_____

_____

had escaped from its enclosure – What did you exclaim and feel when you noticed the monkey trying to escape?

_____

_____

How did its enclosure look? What caused it to escape?

_____

_____

was running through the zoo – What did the monkey do as it ran through the zoo?

_____

_____

Identifying the Technique

Writers use a combination of techniques to elaborate on their writing and make it come alive.

Pick out the words or phrases in each of the following that help you identify the elaboration techniques used. Write the technique used.

1. The children thundered down the hill like a herd of elephants. The dust swirled around them in dusty pink circles, softening the sharp angles of their bony bodies.

Words and / or Phrases	Elaboration Technique

2. Patsy sprinted out of her classroom as soon as the shrill school bell called out the end of day. "Get out of my way!" she mumbled to herself as throngs of students swarmed around the corridors. Forced to slow down, Patsy's thoughts raced ahead of her. She could hardly wait to feel the baby-soft silkiness of the special lace scarf that Aunt Catalina was weaving for her.

Words and / or Phrases	Elaboration Technique

3. She bounded into the house, her tail between her legs, even before the first crash of thunder could be heard. The salty smell of rain hung thick in the air. The fear in her eyes tore at my heart. She leaned her heavy, trembling body against my legs for support. "There, there. It's okay, girl," I cooed softly. Running my fingers through her thick, luxurious coat, I could not believe that a dog, almost the size of an adult man, could be so distressed by a thunderstorm.

Words and / or Phrases	Elaboration Technique

4. Brooke loved chocolates. And what's there not to love? Even before sinking your teeth into one, it is a joy to simply hold a piece between your fingers. Fresh out of the refrigerator, the chocolate is cool and hard. It holds a silent promise of more sensory pleasures. Once the warmth of your fingers reaches the chocolate, it transforms into a yielding, velvety piece of heaven. Luxuriate in its rich bitter sweetness. It is no wonder that the chocolate has been touted as the food of the angels.

Words and / or Phrases	Elaboration Technique

Test Prep Tips

Some standardized tests ask you to write a story, an anecdote, a letter, or other kind of narrative piece. In addition, they may require you to complete the piece of writing within a time limit and without teacher assistance or reference materials. By applying the elaboration techniques you have learned, you should experience greater success in such formal assessment situations.

Here are some tried and true test-taking techniques.

Before you write

* Read all directions carefully and completely.
* Give yourself a few moments to think and plan.
* Narrow your focus.
* Think about your audience.
* Make notes, or use graphic organizers to get started.
* Group ideas that go together. Cross out ideas you do not need.
* Make an organizational plan of how to present your ideas.

Looking back, ask yourself

* Did I make my point clearly and effectively?
* Did I stick to my topic?
* Did I support main ideas with adequate details?
* Do my paragraphs have unity?
* Did I write a winning beginning and a memorable ending?
* Is there anything else I ought to add or delete?
* Did I fix errors in spelling, capitalization, and punctuation?
* Is my handwriting legible?

Common Editing Symbols

Symbol	Description	Example
ஒ	Delete (Take it away forever!)	a ~~tiny~~ kitten
—	Delete and change to something else	sleep all ~~day~~ night
¶	Begin a new paragraph	¶ It was a dark and stormy night.
ⓛⓒ	Lowercase that capital letter	ⓛⓒ A Horse's mane
ⓒⓐⓟ ≡	Capitalize that lowercase letter	ⓒⓐⓟ in Santa Fe, New mexico
⌄	Insert comma	Cheyenne͵Wyoming
ᵛ ᵛ	Insert quotation marks	Carlos asked, ᵛHow are you?ᵛ
⊙	Insert period	An ant ambled about ⊙
?	Insert question mark	Where is Copenhagen?
∿	Transpose (or swap positions)	A cat slipped on the floor waxed.
ⓢⓟ	Check the spelling	ⓢⓟ wether

Self-Prompting Hints

Read your writing out loud. Listen to yourself.

- ❏ Does it sound right?
- ❏ Where could I use a better word?
- ❏ Did I leave out a word or idea?
- ❏ Did I overuse any words?
- ❏ Do I need more supporting details or examples?
- ❏ Could I write an idea more completely?
- ❏ Do my sentences flow smoothly?
- ❏ Does my writing sound interesting?
- ❏ Does every sentence in a paragraph support the main idea?
- ❏ Is there anything that does not belong?

Notice the rise and fall of your voice.

- ❏ If I *stop*, is there a <u>period</u>?
- ❏ If I *pause*, is there a <u>comma</u>?
- ❏ If my voice *rises*, is there a <u>question mark</u>?
- ❏ Do any of my sentences need an <u>exclamation point</u> for *emphasis*?

Read your whole piece of writing.

- ❏ Will it grab and hold a reader's attention?
- ❏ Does the piece paint a picture?
- ❏ Will readers be able to tell the characters apart?
- ❏ Did I vary sentence lengths and types?
- ❏ Did I vary sentence structures and beginnings?
- ❏ Are there parts I can improve by adding figurative language?
- ❏ Is my point of view or opinion clear?
- ❏ Does the dialogue sound like words people really say?
- ❏ Does it have a memorable ending?

Answers

Pages 6-7

A. Things / Animals: Red panda, Bottlenose dolphin, Fennec fox, Shetland pony, Striped dolphin, Red fox
Places: Yellowstone National Park, Central Park, Nature reserve, Art museum, football field, basketball court, tennis court
Persons: lecturer, banker, cab driver, aerobics instructor, referee
Ideas: kindness, strength, pride, integrity

B. Capital cities: Berlin, Beijing, Paris
Landmarks: Eiffel Tower, Great Wall of China
People: Prince William, Mother Teresa, Mr Tenney

C. 1. herd 2. team 3. flock 4. choir 5. gang
6. band

Page 8

A. 1. The rich family lives in a mansion.
2. The chauffeur drives Mr Simpson around in a limousine.
3. They lived on Main Street.
4. Mr Simpson is a music producer.
5. He enjoys working with young singers.

Pages 9-11 *Accept reasonable answers.*

Pages 12-13

A. Qualities: bravery, loyalty, honesty, compassion, courage
Feelings: love, anger, sympathy, hatred, fear
Ideas / Concepts: justice, knowledge, faith, thought, culture

B. 1. friendship 2. confidence 3. honesty
4. brilliance 5. reality 6. wisdom
7. kindness 8. freedom 9. goodness
10. childhood

C. *Accept reasonable answers.*

Pages 14-15

These are suggested answers.
1. I am not at liberty to discuss Lucy's personal matter.
2. Overcome with grief, Nina lost her appetite for food.
3. Write down the address lest your memory fails you.
4. It is a teacher's duty to discipline her students when they misbehave.
5. It is prerequisite for all the candidates to be fluent in Japanese to apply for this position.
6. Many children in the world cannot afford education.

7. Dr Hawks reached the zenith of his chosen field of study at a relatively young age.
8. It was by no accident that Tina got into trouble with Mrs Johnson.
9. The enmity between Malathy and Elaine is well-known.
10. We can taste success only if we persevere.

Pages 16-27 *Accept reasonable answers.*

Pages 28-29

A. M – generously, inward, immediately, jaggedly, offensively, oddly, jokingly, kiddingly, suddenly, well, rapidly
T – yesterday, next
F – always, daily, ever, never, quickly, recently, repeatedly, seldom, monthly, next, usually, yearly
Pp – because, purposely
P – downstairs, home, nearby, outside, somewhere
D – absolutely, almost, bitterly, blissfully, candidly, completely, deliberately, fairly, far, fervently, gleefully, gracefully, highly, inquisitively, inward, joyously, keenly, kind-heartedly, lazily, less, lower, miserably, minutely, nearly, slightly, terribly, thoroughly, too, zealously, zestfully

B. 1. deeply   2. Eventually 3. critically
4. enigmatically 5. tonight 6. most
7. Clearly   8. wrongly

Pages 30-31

A. *Accept reasonable answers.*
B. sadness simply frequently hurriedly fatally exasperatedly magically defiantly carefully boastfully
1. frequently 2. defiantly 3. carefully 4. fatally

Pages 32-36 *Accept reasonable answers.*

Page 37

B. *These are suggested answers.*
1. fortunate, critical   2. crashed
3. seriously   4. upset
5. optimistic, novel   6. vacation
7. famous   8. trips
9. delicacies   10. praised
11. helped   12. heroine

Pages 38–53 *Accept reasonable answers.*

Pages 54–55
A. 1. Man is the only type of animal that can laugh and cry.
2. The appreciative audience cheered on the actors.
3. Everyone in school holds Mr Johnson in high regard.
4. Hospital and health workers are beginning to take laughter seriously.
5. The teachers have taught much since the beginning of the year.
B. 1. a 2. a 3. a 4. b 5. b 6. b 7. a 8. b

Pages 56–57 *Accept reasonable answers.*

Page 58
A. SIGHTS: bright glittery lights, a myriad of colors
SOUNDS: constant chatter of people, clanking of wares   SMELLS: smoky alleys, salty and sweet air
TOUCH: dampness of the night air   TASTES: salty and sweet air

Pages 59–69 *Accept reasonable answers.*

Pages 70–71
A and B. *Accept reasonable answers.*
C. 1. as big as an elephant 2. as black as coal
3. as innocent as a lamb 4. as slippery as an eel
5. as thin as a rake 6. as quiet as a church mouse
7. as cold as ice 8. as pure as snow
9. as free as a bird 10. as steady as a rock

Pages 72–73 *Accept reasonable answers.*

Pages 74–75
A. 1. typewriter = dinosaur, meaning: the typewriter is very old.
2. brother = couch potato, meaning: my brother watches TV all day
3. home = prison, meaning: her home was very restrictive
4. snow = blanket, meaning: the landscape was covered in snow
5. emotions = rollercoaster, meaning: emotional highs and lows
B. *Accept reasonable answers.*

Pages 76–77
A. *These are suggested answers.*
1. Rock means solid. In this case it means that the defender did not let anyone go past him.
2. Sardines in a can means stuffed, crowded or overflowing. Here it means that the vehicle was crowded / packed with passengers.

3. Gushed out means flow out or burst out. In this case it means that the speaker spoke the truth without any inhibition.
4. It means that his father's trust would be broken.
5. To dig up the truth means to find out the truth about anything.
6. It means that someone is furious and no one is being able to reason with her or calm her down.
B and C. *Accept reasonable answers.*

Pages 78–81 *Accept reasonable answers.*

Pages 82–83
A. 1. Pow 2. popped 3. Whack 4. moo 5. splat
6. boom 7. chatter 8. plopped 9. screeched
10. crackled
B. *Accept reasonable answers.*

Pages 84–85
A. 1. C 2. G 3. E 4. F 5. D 6. B 7. H 8. A
B. *These are suggested answers.*
1. To agree with each other.   2. To reveal a secret.
3. To be on the edge of danger.   4. To feel sad.
5. A situation that is not pleasant.   6. A passenger in a car who gives the driver unwanted advice.
7. To work late into the night.   8. To do something in the easiest or cheapest way.   9. To get into trouble.
10. Something good that isn't recognized at first.

Pages 86–87
A. 1. on the same wavelength 2. play devil's advocate
3. long in the tooth 4. Rome was not built in a day
5. necessity is the mother of invention
6. on a fool's errand
B. *Accept reasonable answers.*

Pages 88–89
A. 1. 2 2. 1 3. 1 4. 3 5. 2 6. 1 7. 2 8. 1
9. 3 10. 2
B. 1. carpet 2. dime 3. jump 4. ovation 5. whim
6. lend, hand 7. world 8. price

Pages 90–91
A. *These are suggested answers.*
1. She was stupid.   2. The car can travel very quickly.   3. I have a lot of things to do in a short time.   4. The stench is very strong.   5. My back hurts a lot.   6. It takes her very long to get ready.
7. He adores her and would do anything for her.
B. Accept *reasonable answers.*

Pages 92–123 *Accept reasonable answers.*